KU-059-463

# YOU & YOUR CHILD
# PRE-SCHOOL
# EDUCATION

COPYRIGHT
Every effort has been made to trace copyright holders and to obtain
their permission for the use of copyright material. The authors and
publishers will gladly receive any information enabling them to rectify
any error or omission in subsequent editions.

First published 1999

Letts Educational
Aldine House
Aldine Place
London W12 8AW
Telephone  020 8740 2266

Text: © BPP (Letts Educational) Ltd 1999

Author: Anne Mercer
Series editor: Roy Blatchford
Project manager: Alex Edmonds
Editorial assistance: Tanya Solomons

Design and illustrations: © BPP (Letts Educational) Ltd 1999
Design by Peter Laws
Illustrations by Madeleine Hardy
Cover design by Peter Laws

All our Rights are Reserved. No part of this publication may be
reproduced, stored in a retrieval system, or transmitted, in any form or
by any means, electronic, mechanical, photocopying, recording or
otherwise, without the prior permission of Letts Educational.

British Library Cataloguing in Publication Data
A CIP record for this book is available at the British Library.

ISBN 185758 9769

Colour Reproduction by PDQ Repro Limited, Bungay, Suffolk.
Printed and bound in Italy

Letts Educational is the trading name of BPP (Letts Educational) Ltd

Letts Educational would like to thank all the parents who sent in their tips for educating children
and who wrote with such enthusiasm about parenthood.

# YOU & YOUR CHILD
# PRE-SCHOOL EDUCATION

Anne Mercer

# Contents

Words in **bold** are defined in the glossary at the back of this book.

*"Do not confine your children to your own learning for they were born in different time."*

HEBREW PROVERB

**Dear Parent,**

What happens at nursery and in primary school is vital to your child's education. What you do at home is just as important.

It's never too soon to start supporting your child's learning. The time that you spend with your child during the first months and years gives him or her a foundation that will last a lifetime. Make the most of every opportunity for you and your child to enjoy learning together.

You don't need to be an expert. You do need to be enthusiastic. The time you invest at home – playing, talking and listening – will help your child achieve throughout pre-school, right up to secondary school and beyond.

This book is one in a major new series from Letts. It will help you support your child, with information about learning at home and at pre-school. It tells you how these places organise children's learning, and how you can best prepare and encourage your child.

Enjoy sharing your child's first experiences of pre-school. The important thing is to make learning fun!

*Roy Blatchford.*

ROY BLATCHFORD
*Series editor*

# Choosing a place for your child's pre-school education

## What is available?

Pre-school provision varies greatly across Britain and it can be state funded or private. For children between the ages of three and five, the two main kinds of pre-school are playgroups and nurseries. Many four-year-olds are also included in primary school Reception classes.

### PLAYGROUPS

Playgroups offer **Early Years** experiences in informal settings, organised by staff with less academic training. Parents will also be involved, often on a rota basis, as part of the staff. Parental involvement is expected in playgroups that belong to the **Pre-school Learning Alliance (PLA)**. Playgroups stress play and social skills as a learning priority.

### NURSERY SCHOOLS

Nursery schools and classes usually have a more formal and structured organisation, requiring staff with teaching qualifications as well as staff trained in childcare. Nurseries may be private or state run, and both sectors have a recognisable curriculum designed for Early Years learning.

### RECEPTION CLASSES

Four-year-olds in Reception classes within a primary school should be offered a special early years curriculum. Learning through practical activity should be a major part of the day. Teachers should have been trained in Early Years education and development.

# What makes a good playgroup?

✔ The environment should be happy and caring.

✔ There should be opportunities for interesting play.

✔ There should be opportunities to mix and socialise with other children and adults.

✔ Activities should extend the play opportunities children are offered by toys and materials available to them at home.

**Parent tip**

"Visit the establishment – observe the children at play and the reactions of the teachers or carers to the children."

### Learning through play

Any organisation offering pre-school education should have a large emphasis on 'learning through play' and activities involving lots of adult-child interaction and conversation. Early Years children need activity and talk. Parents should be welcome in an Early Years environment. If not, be wary !

# What is the best setting for my child?

To decide the best place for your child, think about which one will best meet his or her needs, and the needs of your family. Arrange to visit several different places. Consider the following questions:

> **Routines**
>
> Very young children are secure when they have a regular routine and know where everything belongs. This is equally important in environments outside the home.

Q  Is your child very active with a short concentration span?

A  Choose a pre-school environment with plenty of space and lots of safe outdoor equipment. Make sure that children are given opportunities to move between activities quite often. Consider whether staff cope happily with demanding children.

Q  Does your child learn quickly and need further stimulation? Is your child very demanding?

A  Children who learn quickly are very demanding because they need to be shown ways of using what they learn and frequently presented with new ideas. A nursery with trained teaching staff may be better able to cope with providing more demanding learning activities in line with the child's age.

Q  Does your child have any physical problems, or speech and language problems?

A  Choose a place for your child where staff are well trained in Early Years education and can use assessment and planning to help your child develop successfully. Nursery classes are more likely to have support from specialists, including the Gifted and Able Service of the **Local Education Authority (LEA)**.

**Q** Do you feel comfortable about leaving your child regularly in the chosen pre-school?

**A** Discussing worries and problems with parents who have the same concerns helps to put your mind at rest without having to face the professional staff until you know them better.

**Q** Do you know other families who will be using the same playgroup or nursery?

**A** Talk to them about how their children settled in and what problems they had. Perhaps they can reassure you about any particular worries you have about the group.

**Q** Is support and friendship offered to parents, including fathers or other carers, as well as to children?

**A** Many nurseries have drop-in rooms for adults. There may be workshops to help parents learn about play, behaviour, language and so on. Find out if the staff greet and speak to everyone to make them feel welcomed.

**Q** Is parent help welcomed?

**A** A good pre-school education sees a child's learning as part of social development and promotes a partnership between home and playgroup or nursery. Pre-schools which welcome parents to take part in pre-school activities not only support those parents in helping their children's learning, but benefit from special talents or expertise parents may have to offer.

**Q** Who will be collecting your child?

**A** Consider how many hours your child will be there, and any problems concerning journeys to and from the pre-school. Most pre-schools are very strict about being informed if someone different is collecting a child.

**Q** How much will it cost?

**A** Whether the pre-school is state funded or charges a fee may be an issue if you are paying for other childcare.

## WHAT CHILDREN SAY

"I like playgroup because I can play with lots of toys."

"When we come we learn things and we'll be able to go to big school."

# Where to get information about pre-school education

For information about what is available nationally write to the **Department for Education and Employment (DfEE)** or the **British Association for Early Childhood Education**; Her Majesty's Stationery Office (HMSO) will provide booklets of relevant information. These organisations may also have information on the Internet.

For local information use your library, telephone directories and advertisements in supermarkets, newsagents, local papers or any older sibling's school. The headteacher of your local infant school may also be happy to make a recommendation, but be careful to contact him or her at a convenient time – usually after class hours.

The local Education Office will usually produce a book of information about all the education it provides, including Local Education Authority (LEA) nursery classes and special nurseries, so that you can contact these direct. The Early Years Advisor may also be able to help.

Some private nurseries may promote learning according to particular philosophies, for example Montessori schools, Froebbel kindergartens or Headstart.

> **Professional tip**
>
> Always check that nurseries or playgroups have adequate insurance and are supervised through educational or social services inspections. All staff working with children should be vetted by the local authority and/or the police.

*Finally, don't forget to ask other parents!*

# Visiting nursery schools or playgroups

Before making a decision about where to place your child, ask if you can visit some pre-school organisations in your area. Contact the playgroup leader or nursery teacher first and ask for a brochure or printed information – reading this may help you think of questions you would like to ask or answer any worries in advance.

## WHEN VISITING A PLAYGROUP OR NURSERY, ASK YOURSELF THESE QUESTIONS:

• Are the people friendly? Can we be shown around and introduced to children and adults?

• Are there quiet areas as well as play areas. It is particularly important to have a place where children can rest.

• Is the room well organised and safe, with access to safe and supervised outdoor play?

• Do the children seem happy and involved with their activities?

• Can parents stay and join in activities?

• Are there enough adults for the number of children?

## THINGS CHILDREN LIKE TO KNOW

- *Where are the toilets?*

When you are at an age where accidents can happen with the slightest delay, easy access to the toilets is essential. Children engrossed in play can often leave getting to the toilet to the last minute.

- *Can I choose?*

Children need to know exactly what they can and can't do to feel secure. It must be made clear when they can do things for themselves and when it is expected they will do as they are told.

- *Have I got my lunch?*

Children can get very distressed if they don't understand what is happening at meal times. Food is very important when you are small and get hungry quickly.

- *Where do things go?*

Little children have a sense of security when they know that everything is in its right place. It is important that staff encourage children to tidy up and show them where things belong.

• *When do things happen?*
Clear, regular routines also add to a child's sense of
security in a strange place.

• *Who will tell me what to do?*
Sometimes it is not obvious to children who is a
member of staff and who is a helper. Make sure
there is a clear structure that the adults in the
pre-school stick to. Ideally, staff should handle
all matters of discipline. There should also be
guidelines on how children should behave
towards adults.

• *Do adults have time to listen to me?*
Pre-school organisation and staffing should allow lots of opportunities
for adults to stop and listen carefully when children have something to
talk to them about. They should encourage conversation, particularly
with children who are nervous.

• *Will I be with my friends?*
Most pre-school staff recognise the great importance children put on
being with friends. Check that any groupings or use of different rooms
takes into account children's concerns about being with other children
they feel happy with. But, remember, not all friendships bring out the
best in children and children should be encouraged to make new friends.

## WHAT TO ASK PRE-SCHOOL STAFF

• What sort of training and qualifications do adults working in the nursery or playgroup have?

• Are outdoor as well as indoor areas secure and adequately supervised?

• What sort of activities are available to the children each session?

• What are the first-aid procedures, and what happens if your child is taken ill or has an accident?

• Can I talk to parents who already have children at the establishment?

• How do staff manage children leaving at the end of the session to ensure they are met by the right person?

• How do staff deal with naughty children?

• Are refreshments provided?

# What information will I find in a playgroup or nursery brochure?

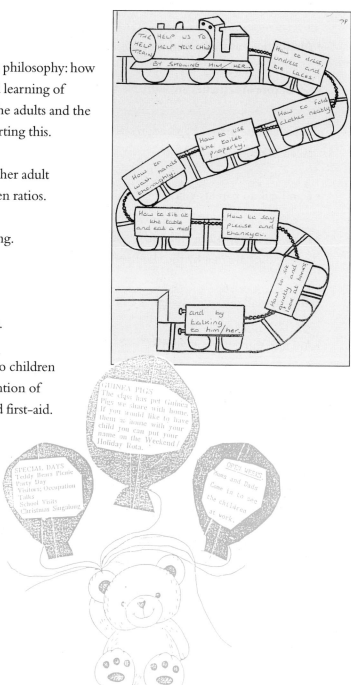

- A statement of the pre-school's philosophy: how they view the development and learning of young children and what part the adults and the environment will play in supporting this.

- Some description of the staff, other adult involvement and staff-to-children ratios.

- The style of learning and teaching.

- What activities are available.

- Some description of equipment.

- What special areas are available to children indoors and out, with some mention of policies for health and safety, and first-aid.

- Descriptions of any outside visits made and staffing for these.

- Maintenance of good behaviour and discipline procedures.

# What about Dad?

Many more pre-schools recognise that fathers, especially those who are the sole parent, may not feel included in an Early Years environment. Good pre-schools try to address this problem. The involvement of men provides a more balanced learning experience for all children.

## What teachers say

"We make an effort to talk to fathers when they bring children at the beginning of a session, just as we do to mothers. A member of staff waits at the door to greet everyone."

"We ask fathers if they would like to come in and help once a week, just like mothers."

"Just like mothers, fathers may have special skills they can bring to the pre-school, like an interest in gardening, or an interesting job, like producing books."

# Starting pre-school

## Preparing your child to start

The most important advice given by parents and staff working with young children is that by the time they start pre-school, children should be as independent and confident as possible. The process of becoming independent and confident – in learning in new situations and in meeting new people – is continued throughout the pre-school stage and in the Reception class.

Many parents often feel guilty about sending their children to pre-school and sharing the care of their children with someone else. They sometimes also feel jealous of their child's relationship with their key worker or teacher, and can be upset when they first start. Parents can be more upset than the children.

Remember your child will take his or her cues from you, so keep smiling. This is your child's first adventure into the social world he or she must grow up in. It can be a really happy and informal preparation for the bigger step he or she will take at the start of primary school.

### Parent tip

"In the months prior to your child starting pre-school, help him or her to become as self-sufficient and independent as possible – seeing to his or her own toileting needs, being able to put on a coat and shoes on. Don't over-mother them. Life is to be enjoyed; discovering new things is exciting."

By the time children start pre-school they should:

- be able to go to the toilet on their own
- know how to wash and dry their hands on their own
- be able to put their coat and shoes on themselves and be learning how to fasten them
- be able to stop and listen when they are spoken to
- be able to sit still for short periods and concentrate on an activity such as completing a jigsaw or making a Stickle Brick model

Demands for constant adult attention should be discouraged – children should be able to occupy themselves for short periods. Make sure your child is able to share during play activities with you. Turn-taking games are good for developing social skills.

It is important that children mix with other children and adults from an early age.

## Turn-taking activities

✔ Snakes and ladders
✔ Hop scotch
✔ Snap
✔ Very simple dice
✔ Games involving counting
✔ I Spy
✔ Shooting goals

## Parent tips

"Have confidence in the nursery and try not to think about it while you are at work, or doing things at home."

"Get your child involved at an early age in mixing with other children, for example at toddler groups. "

"Leave your child with a familiar relation or friend sometimes so they realise other adults – apart from parents – can take care of their needs. Reading books about pre-school with them also helps."

"When leaving your child at pre-school, emphasise that you will be back soon."

"Show them on a clock face what time you will be back."

"My child is able to wave to me through the window – this makes her happy."

# Be positive

Having decided to send your child to a
pre-school, always be very positive about it.
You will feel most positive if you have
found out as much as you can about the
nursery or playgroup and have discussed
any concerns with the staff. Visiting
beforehand – with your child – to explore
the new activities he or she will encounter
is very important.

Many pre-schools send staff to meet
parents and children in their own homes. A
new adult is less threatening to children on
home ground, and there will be a familiar
face when they start. Often this staff
member will be a key worker – a particular
member of staff who will always be there to
welcome your child and be responsible for
his or her care and assessment. Pre-school
will seem much more familiar if the key
worker tells your child what kind of
activities he or she will be involved in.

## Parent tips

"Get them involved in an activity as soon
as they get into the school. Let them
bring a familiar toy with them."

"Get children there on time and don't be
late collecting them."

"A regular routine every morning helps."

"Be open-minded. What you like might
not be best for your child – think about
your child's needs."

"The new intake was spread over the first
month so that younger children got used
to their surroundings in a small group."

"Parents were able to stay for a while – as
long as they wanted."

"The number of hours my child stayed
was gradually increased."

"The nursery teacher greets every child
as he or she arrives and distracts children
who start to get upset by taking them to
an activity such as the sandpit."

# Dealing with tears

Most teachers will tell you that it pays to remember to kiss your child and say good-bye. If this gets forgotten in the rush, even the most independent become tearful. No child is upset for very long after a parent has left – if children are frequently distressed for longer than a few minutes they may not be emotionally developed enough for pre-school education.

## Parent tips and quotes

"Get him or her excited about going by explaining the routine and what to can look forward to."

"Get a story book about going to nursery or playgroup. Make the situation sound familiar."

"The teacher from my daughter's nursery came to our home to visit and she brought photos of the children engaged in different activities. That really gave Jason confidence because he got excited about meeting all the other children."

# The Early Years curriculum and assessment

'Curriculum' is a word that can worry parents and teachers alike. For Early Years children it means quite simply the activities, rules and ways of learning that are presented to them. Attitudes to behaviour, individual needs, multi-cultural issues and developing relationships with others are part of this. A curriculum based on subjects like English or maths (**The National Curriculum**) will not apply until your child is older.

> **Parent tip**
>
> "Go to a toddler group or Tumble Tots session so your child gets used to being with other children."

Assessment is also part of the curriculum. It is part of the staff planning that ensures children enjoy a broad range of activities suited to their individual learning.

Assessment does not mean tests or written exercises. It is mostly informal – the staff observing children while they are playing or busy with activities.

A short note or tick list may be used occasionally to test your child. If he or she comes to pre-school able to hold a pencil correctly and write his or her name, the activities presented will need to go on from this starting point – playing with letter shapes and opportunities to learn letter formation and sounds. Another child who has no experience of drawing or writing will need different activities to widen his or her experience.

Making an assessment of each child's needs is important to good teaching and learning. It enables staff to inform you about your child's progress and you can find out what you can do to help with learning and play at home.

# Early Years Outcomes

Most pre-school organisations plan their curriculum around activities designed to help children achieve the nationally agreed Desirable Learning Outcomes for five-year-olds. These are:

## 1. PERSONAL AND SOCIAL DEVELOPMENT

Children should be able to:

- listen and concentrate
- share and co-operate with others
- show independence in things like dressing themselves

> **Example of Activity**
> A snakes and ladders board game in which the children must concentrate on the board to count the spaces correctly, co-operate in a group taking turns fairly and accept winning or losing. The teacher can sometimes hand on the dice out of turn so that children have an opportunity to talk about 'being fair'.

## 2. LANGUAGE AND LITERACY

Children should be able to:

- understand how books work
- listen and respond to stories, rhymes, songs and poems
- make up their own stories and enjoy role play
- know some sounds and letters
- draw pictures and start to write some letters and symbols in play writing

> **Example of Activity**
> Sharing a 'big book' containing print and pictures with an adult in a group. The adult shows how print is read from left to right, what a picture is, what the words are, and how to read through a book. Children will learn new vocabulary from the story.

## 3.MATHEMATICS

Children should begin to:

- use mathematical language, such as 'circle', 'in front of', 'bigger than' and 'more', to describe shape, position, size and quantity

- recognise and make patterns

- become familiar with number rhymes, songs, stories, counting games and activities

- understand and record numbers, and begin to show awareness of addition and subtraction

---

**Example of Activity**

To develop mathematical language, the teacher moves a bear to different places in the room. She asks the children to tell her where it is using phrases such as 'on top of', 'behind', 'below' and 'between'.

---

## 4.KNOWLEDGE AND UNDERSTANDING OF THE WORLD

Children learn about events in their own lives. They also look at living and man-made things in both the place where they live and outside the home. They begin to explore how things are made and how they work.

---

**Example of Activity**

Making a 'time line' helps children to understand the sequence of 'time' which is a very hard concept for them. Using photographs of the children as babies, the teacher asks them to draw themselves as babies, toddlers and present day. These are pegged on a line in order, and the children asked what they could do at each age. A timeline of events through the day may also be used.

---

## 5.PHYSICAL DEVELOPMENT

Children are encouraged to move confidently and imaginatively with increasing control and co-ordination. An awareness of space and other people, using balancing and climbing apparatus, balls and skipping ropes is also developed. They should know how to handle tools, objects, building blocks and playdough materials safely and with increasing control.

---

**Example of Activity**

Outdoor play on large apparatus like climbing frames, tunnels, bikes and pedal cars. Indoor play with small apparatus – threading beads or buttons, jigsaws, construction kits like Duplo, Lego or Stickle Bricks, cutting out.

---

## 6.CREATIVE DEVELOPMENT

Children should explore sound and colour, texture, shape, form and space in art and craft and music. Through art, music, dance, stories and imaginative play, they learn to use their imagination, to listen and to observe, and to use their senses to help them respond.

---

**Example of Activity**

The range of activities creative pre-school staff can design and plan for your child is endless. It is likely to include painting, making 'junk models' and collage pictures, listening to music tapes and using percussion instruments. Once you have visited the pre-school and seen what activities they arrange, you will soon be able to think of more of your own.

---

# How are pre-schools run?

To be a nursery rather than a playgroup, a pre-school must have a qualified nursery teacher and a nursery nurse, and a ratio of one adult to 13 children. In a playgroup, where staff may be less qualified, the ratio is one adult to eight children. The Pre-school Learning Alliance runs courses to qualify their playleaders and volunteer helpers in learning through play.

Your child's key worker in pre-school will be the member of staff who has particular responsibility for and knowledge of him or her. A key worker should know the children he or she is responsible for very well and work most frequently with them. It is the key worker who will assess your child's progress.

## FUNDING AND INSPECTION

Some pre-schools are funded entirely by fees from parents. Most receive funds from local authorities under provisions set up under the now revised Voucher Scheme.

Pre-schools receiving Voucher Scheme payments are inspected by OFSTED (Office for Standards in Education ). All nurseries and playgroups are subject to LEA policies on health and safety and child protection. Those outside the state sector are inspected by social services each year.

**Parent quote**

"My son's key worker came to welcome him every morning and took him to play with other children. That really helped him to feel that he fitted in and to overcome any nervousness he felt."

# Parents concerns

*"I worry about safety on the premises and in the gardens, and the proper screening of teachers."*

Security has two aspects:

**1)** Security of the buildings and play areas to make sure that children cannot wander off, and that visitors are all checked in and have only one point of entry during sessions.

**2)** The vetting of all staff and adults working with children through checking against the LEA checklist of offenders, social services, education and police records.

*"What do staff do with naughty children?"*

Behaviour is very much part of the pre-school learning process. It is behaviour that is naughty, not the child. To encourage good behaviour the pre-school should have a behaviour policy that ensures consistent management of the children by all staff and helpers. Praise and rewards, like extra playing time, special choosing privileges, stickers or stars should encourage positive social skills and help children understand the rules.

Unwanted behaviour should be discouraged by a calm, negative response – ignoring, removing or distracting the child from the problem. Alternatively, the teacher may use **'time out'**. This means sitting the child away from other children with a member of staff who does not respond to him or her for five minutes – a calming process.

*"Can you talk to the teacher about any concerns immediately or does an appointment have to be made?"*

Complaints procedures vary from pre-school to pre-school. It's a good idea to ask about this when your child first starts. Try to speak to the staff concerned to get facts straight. Your complaint should be taken seriously and dealt with quickly, confidentially and sensitively.

*"Do all children have equal opportunities within the pre-school?"*

Questions that you need to consider include: Are boys and girls encouraged to take part in all activities and act out different roles in their play? Are some activities related to different cultures, religions and festivals? Do staff have a positive attitude to meeting the needs of children from different cultures or races, or those with disabilities?

*"If a child requires regular medication, such as an inhaler, will the staff administer it?"*

Health and safety procedures will cover such things as how medications are given to children and first-aid training for staff.

**Additional areas include:**
- Are there physical routines such as hand washing and toilet training?
- Is there a safe area to change children?
- Are refreshments and snacks provided?
- Is there supervision over handling of pets?
- Is hygiene taken into account when playing with playdough or sand and water?
- Is there a quiet area for tired children, or children taken ill, to rest?
- Are there routines for ensuring children leave with the right person at the end of sessions?
- Does the school have fire drills?

*"What facilities and activities will be provided?"*

This can depend on the layout of the pre-school and whether it is using premises like a church or village hall. You need to think about the inside and outside areas as well as what toilet facilities there are and whether they are designed for children. Are adaptations like steps needed and are there wheelchair ramps, wide toilets or wider doors available if needed for children with **special needs**?

> ### Parent tip
>
> "It is important that there are activities going on when children arrive, so that they can join in with them and not feel shy or embarrassed waiting to play with other children."

## ALL PRE-SCHOOLS SHOULD PROVIDE A RICH ENVIRONMENT AND WILL HAVE AREAS FOR:

- ✔ active play (climbing equipment, balls, bikes)

- ✔ 'messy' or wet play, such as sand and water

- ✔ quiet areas like a book corner or 'listening' with headphones

- ✔ a mark making area where children draw, colour and make their first steps in writing with chalk and paint or pens

- ✔ a construction area where children play with building sets, bricks and Lego

- ✔ an area for imaginative play where there will be a dolls' house, dolls and toy cars

- ✔ a role play area with dressing-up clothes

# Moving from pre-school to Reception class

Most primary school Reception classes arrange an induction meeting or day to meet new children and their parents. Sometimes this is arranged through your child's pre-school if it has links with the primary school. You will be able to:-

- meet the teachers and assistant staff
- see your child's new classroom
- look at information about the school day and new routines
- see displays of early maths, English and science work and equipment

# Baseline Assessment

Within the first seven weeks of starting Reception, the teacher will watch the children performing simple classroom tasks. This is called **Baseline Assessment**. It enables teachers to make judgements about your child's knowledge and development when he or she starts formal education. It will show you what your child has learned from his or her pre-school experiences. Teaching can be planned from this starting point. The assessments cover the areas of:

- reading
- writing
- speaking and listening
- mathematics
- personal and social development

It is expected that, during their fifth year, most children will be able to achieve the Early Years Outcomes described in Chapter Three.

*"Children who have had a good pre-school education – at home or outside it – have a head start."*

## What the experts say

What is certain is that the Early Years matter, whether you choose to have your child at home full-time or place her or him in a pre-school group. Parents should never under-estimate the great influence they have during their child's vital early years.

### Professional quote

"We know that children who benefit from nursery education are more likely to succeed in primary school." *(Excellence in Schools, DfEE, 1997)*

"At long last the crucial importance of good quality Early Years education is finally being recognised. Research evidence that children's success in school and other aspects of their life can be significantly enhanced by quality experiences when they are very young is being taken seriously." *(Teaching and Learning in the Early Years by David Whitbread, Routledge, 1998)*

# Play and language

## What do we mean by play ?

**A**dults often see play as the opposite of work – a treat after work has been done. But in the development of young children play has a different meaning. Children under six years old learn in a different way from adults and older children.

✔ Play is your child's work.

✔ Play is your child's way of finding out about things.

✔ In play, your child can practise skills he or she has learned without any pressure.

---

### Children in action

A child playing with building blocks will be exploring the feeling of the wood, the colours, the space they cover and how they can be put together. After building in lots of different ways he or she might come to the conclusion that the tower will stand up best with the big bricks at the bottom. The child has learned a lot about balance and shape which he or she will bring to maths and physics lessons later in life. If an adult joins in to talk about what is happening, the child will also learn lots of useful language – big and small, what the shapes and colours are called, words like 'balancing' and what they mean.

## Play is a natural activity for us all. We learn by doing.

Research into learning has shown that we all remember new things much better if we are shown how to do them and can have a go ourselves. Just reading, or being told instructions, set apart from the activity, makes remembering the activity much harder.

We have all seen situations where young children seem not to know what to do with toys and equipment. They may keep bringing the toy to an adult and asking about it or repeat what it is over and over. This is a stage babies and toddlers go through. Being able to play in a positive way, choosing and creating games, has to be shown to children.

In pre-school there should be a balance between child-initiated play and play that is guided by adults. You can keep this balance at home by sometimes leaving your child to his or her own devices, at other times suggesting play or joining in yourself.

### Teacher's tip

"The most effective way to teach Early Years children is through structured play."

## PLAY IS STRUCTURED WHEN:

- what the children can learn from the play is planned beforehand

- what the children can learn has been decided on the basis of what they can do already

- equipment, toys and apparatus have been well chosen and are readily on hand

- sufficient space and time are made available for the activity to take place and be worthwhile

- an adult is on hand to help children learn and practise language skills

- the adult can think of new ways to play with the skills learned

# The importance of talking

All play begins with an exploration stage – children will want to handle toys and equipment, move them about and find out what they do. When children play like this you may hear them make sounds, talk or sing to themselves. In the same way that children explore physical things they explore language.

*Learning language gives your child a tool for thinking and being creative. A lively imagination is achieved when ideas can be put into words.*

There is increasing evidence that a growing number of young children have speech and language difficulties. One of the most important things parents can do to prepare children for pre-school is to spend lots of time listening, talking and playing with them.

## Communication skills

Play is the opportunity for your child to talk with adults and other children. It is important for children to play alongside others of the same age who share similar communication skills. For example, if you listen to children at the pre-school, you may hear them repeat words and phrases used by adults. This is a way of practising language they have learned from listening. Children who don't quite get the words or sentence structure right will usually be corrected by more capable classmates.

# Helping your child

When you are playing or talking with your child, reduce background noise such as traffic, the TV or kitchen appliances. Young children do not distinguish sounds as easily as we do. Play a listening game, set a time and listen for how many sounds you can hear. Ask your child to stay quiet while you say a nursery rhyme. See how much of the rhyme your child can remember or whether he or she can hear words that sound the same – the rhymes.

Take every opportunity to increase your child's vocabulary and use of language. When out shopping, in the car, walking or going to school, talk to your child about what he or she can see. Make up lists out loud, ask questions and prompt the answers, tell your child how to say the words correctly – you may need to help at first. When your child is playing, ask him or her about the game.

## Parent tip

"You don't have to spend lots of money to help children develop good play and language skills – skills which will help them enormously in a pre-school."

# Pasta activity

This play activity teaches colour words, sorting colours and improves hand-eye co-ordination.

You will need different sorts of hollow pasta, a selection of food colouring, some wool and a darning needle, or stiff string for use without a needle.

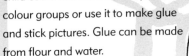

Dye handfuls of the pasta different colours using the food dyes and cold water. Dry them on kitchen roll. Show your child how to thread them on the wool to make bracelets of different colours or in different patterns, for example red, blue, yellow. This is a maths activity that teaches your child to recognise repeating patterns. Tell your child the colour words and talk about what you are doing as you go along. Your child could sort the left-over pasta into colour groups or use it to make glue and stick pictures. Glue can be made from flour and water.

## Tour activity

Take your child on a walk around the house or somewhere interesting in the local area. Explain that you are going to see how many shapes and coloured things you can find. Relate colours and shapes to objects, for example a red cylinder is a post box, a grey circle is a manhole cover, a blue rectangle is a door.

## Salt writing

This play activity involves using the left-to-right eye movements necessary for reading and writing. It also involves pattern making, forming letters and numbers and learning what they are called, as well as developing the sense of touch.

You will need a baking tray covered in flour or salt. Put newspaper over the floor and table where you are doing the activity to avoid mess. Children need to learn about this too. Show your child how to draw patterns in the flour or salt using the index finger moving from left to right. Talk about how it feels. After your child has had time to experiment alone, show him or her how to write numbers and letters in the tray – naming them as you write them.

# A play checklist

Children should be able to do the following at playgroup or nursery:

- ✔ Your child should play happily alongside other children and co-operate with them in their games.

- ✔ Your child should be able to stay at one activity for a short time without constantly demanding someone's attention.

*Remember – keep talking with your child and listening too!*

# Language checklist

✔ Your child should be able to speak in simple sentences to make his or her needs known.

✔ Your child should be confident about speaking to other children and adults in the nursery once he or she gets to know them.

✔ Your child should be able to name many common objects.

✔ Your child should understand what is said to him or her and be able to respond.

If your child has difficulty in these areas of speech and language talk to the pre-school staff about how the pre-school will be able to help, and ask them for suggestions for activities to do at home. Check that your child's hearing is okay or ask about being referred to a speech and language therapist to see if there is a particular problem.

> **Parent quote**
>
> "My child was always demanding attention at home – watching the sort of activities children did at pre-school gave me lots of ideas for things to do at home. Some toys he couldn't do much with, so I was more careful about what I bought in toy shops too."

# How can pre-schools support parents?

The nursery or playgroup can be a source of information about

✔ activities for children in your area, for example story-telling at your local library

✔ medical concerns, such as meningitis or 'nits'

✔ common worries parents may have about their children, for example biting or not sharing

In addition, many schools have 'drop in rooms' where parents can have coffee and meet one another. Information leaflets are available and sometimes tapes, videos and books for loan. Some pre-schools arrange visits from support service staff too – the speech therapist or school nurse for example. Playgroups or nurseries may also have access to a toy library, or loan books or toys of their own for home use.

You may be sent 'paired activities' (games or sheets with activity suggestions) to do at home. These will be selected at the right learning level for your child.

---

**Parent quote**

"Having taken on the care of a young step-child with difficult behaviour, I was completely unaware of what to expect from a four-year-old. Being invited to parent workshops at the nursery school and being able to watch other children and talk to other parents about problems helped me to cope."

# Other support systems

### SERVING ON THE PLAYGROUP OR NURSERY COMMITTEE

Playgroups or nurseries may have a committee of staff and parents with an elected chairperson that is responsible for the organisation and running of the pre-school, as well as selection of staff. If the nursery is run by private management or a governing body, a parents' committee may meet for the sole purpose of organising fundraising events.

### WORKSHOPS AND COURSES TO SUPPORT CHILDREN'S LEARNING AND PARENTING SKILLS

Workshops may be run by the pre-school staff or by outside professionals, such as the health team, the learning or behavioural support teams from the local authority, an educational psychologist or early years organisations. The style of the workshops may vary from an informal exhibition of apparatus and play equipment for 'hands on' discussion to videos, discussion groups and more formal 'talks'. Workshops dealing with specific problems, for example behaviour, may allow opportunities for one-to-one work with a member of the professional team. If your child's pre-school does not run workshops there are other organisations that have courses for parents and helpers where you can meet other childcare workers and parents.

### ARRANGE FOR A MEMBER OF THE NURSERY STAFF TO VISIT YOUR HOME

Home visits are usually part of the process of starting pre-school when advice and support about helping your child's learning is most relevant. Remember, staff have lots of experience with young children to draw on to help with any queries concerning your child.

# Does your child need extra help?

## What are special educational needs?

Definitions of special educational needs may vary slightly from pre-school to pre-school, school to school, local authority to local authority. This is because staff have detailed knowledge of the particular children in their school or area. However, any child who needs extra help and support to develop his or her learning beyond that given to other mainstream children of the same age is said to have special educational needs.

> **Parent tip**
>
> "Consider what your child's needs are before sending him or her anywhere and visit schools you are considering – with your child – as often as possible beforehand."

# Areas of special need

- children who are gifted or able in one or more areas of learning
- children who are physically disabled
- children with speech or language difficulties, such as dyslexia
- children suffering from visual impairment
- behavioural problems such as shyness/naughtyness.
- children who lack co-ordination in construction/drawing and writing (dyspraxia)
- bereaved or emotionally disturbed children

Some problems concerning reading and word recognition are not readily apparent until a child begins formal education. Baseline Assessment in the reception class provides an indication of possible educational difficulties or the need for extension activities for bright children.

Children who do not have English as a first language may often have difficulty mixing with other children and understanding what they are being asked to do – although they may not actually have special needs. They often have problems seeking help from staff. The pre-school should provide a welcoming and understanding atmosphere for them.

### Teacher definitions of special needs

Here are some definitions from teachers:

"Any child who has a disability or handicap that prevents him or her performing to their full potential – this can be temporary (such as the effects of bereavement orabuse)."

"Children with some sort of requirement (educational, emotional, medical) who need extra teaching time or expertise."

"Any type of child requiring any individual provision to cater adequately for their particular developmental needs, i.e. gifted children, children with physical, emotional or educational problems."

### Parent quote

"Our child has special needs and is supported on a one-to-one basis. He is very secure and happy to be left in an environment that he feels secure in."

# Who can identify special educational needs?

For very young children, medical, developmental, speech or visual problems will most usually be discovered by health visitor checks or at clinic visits. The family doctor may also be involved. Parents themselves may become aware that their child has a particular problem or is very talented in some areas. Never underestimate your knowledge of your child.

> **Parent quote**
>
> "When Robin was identified as having special needs, our concern was whether there were more special one-to-one lessons for children with learning difficulties."

Experiences at pre-school may be the first time talents or problems are spotted. Playgroup and nursery staff play an important part in identifying special needs as early as possible. Good assessment of children's abilities is really important.

Don't panic if staff suggest that your child may need some extra support or specialist help (e.g. speech therapy). Remember – support at the pre-school stage may mean your child has fewer problems when he or she starts school where one-to-one help is less available.

*Special educational needs are often temporary or short-term.*

The Government recognises the great importance of early intervention and a partnership with parents to achieve this. Early Years Development Partnerships have been established in every local authority. These encourage a better flow of information to parents of young children and to find out what their needs are. Most agencies that support children with special needs – such as the Learning Support Service – will be part of the local authority's provision. The LEA officer who manages special educational needs services may be contacted to provide information about which agency will be best able to help your child.

## IF YOUR CHILD HAS SPECIAL NEEDS:

✔ be positive: if a problem is identified it can be tackled

✔ give your child lots of praise and encouragement

✔ support the nursery or playgroup staff in their efforts to help your child

✔ talk about any worries or special concerns with staff as soon as possible

✔ make sure staff know any circumstances that will affect the sort of help they can give your child

There are a whole range of organisations, charities and support groups that give help and information about specific problems. Pre-school staff or parents can contact these. One of the advantages of these organisations is that they can offer advice to parents 'outside the system'. The addresses of some of these organisations are in the back of this book.

## Twins and triplets

Twins or triplets may have special problems – sometimes not mixing with others or having language difficulties. These need to be dealt with early.

## What to ask staff if your child has special needs

Q Is there a member of staff who has training in special education or who has special responsibility for this?

A In nursery departments attached to primary schools there will be a **special educational needs co-ordinator (SENCO)** who will have some special knowledge and training in this area. The SENCO will support staff, children and parents.

Q If my child has a medical or physical condition, can I be sure that staff will act promptly in a crisis?

A Talk to staff about your worries and what experience they have. Make sure you give them lots of information.

Q Will you be fully involved in and informed about special support given to your child?

A Talk to staff again about what support they can provide and whether it is relevant and sufficient for your child.

# Case studies

Three-year-old Stevie is extremely short-sighted, has virtually no spoken vocabulary and cannot co-ordinate movement in his legs and arms. Before starting in a nursery class he had been in the care of an educational psychologist who used a special programme to help him. The aim was to develop independence skills like dressing, washing hands and so on. Stevie also made regular visits to a speech therapist who used toys and games to develop his language 'in conversation'.

## ACTION

With advice from the educational psychologist and speech therapist the nursery class could continue these programmes quite naturally in their play activities. Other children were encouraged to play alongside and talk to Stevie so that he had models to copy. The staff helped Stevie to use the large climbing apparatus and bikes so that he improved his co-ordination. Regular advice about Stevie's progress was given to staff by the school's trained special needs co-ordinator.

## CASE 2. THE ABLE CHILD

Rosie is an extremely bright four-year-old who learns everything very quickly. Like many bright children of this age, Rosie is not so happy at 'choosing time' when she has to decide what play activities to join in with. She much prefers adult direction and formal learning situations. Rosie is an exceptionally able reader who often chooses to sit on her own in the book corner. Unfortunately, this has led to her isolation in the group, and complaints that nobody wants to play with her.

### ACTION

In this case, the pre-school class teacher has to develop Rosie's social skills by intervening in group play, showing Rosie how to listen to other children as well as adults. Other children often like being read to or sharing books with other children, so this special talent can be used to help Rosie relate to her classmates. It is also important that Rosie's teacher makes sure that her ability to read does not outstrip the skills which go hand-in-hand with this – comprehension, spelling and writing. Rosie's concentration on reading may mean that she avoids creative activities and these are also important to early development.

# Early learning at home

Throughout this guide to pre-school education the importance of the school-home partnership has been stressed. There are many different ways of supporting your child's education. This section looks at developing the more formal learning skills needed for English and mathematics.

## How children learn

The human brain has areas on the right and left sides that control different types of learning – **spatial awareness**, imagination and creativity, language and reasoning.

Activities which help the two sides of the brain to function together are very appropriate in the early years when one side may be more dominant than the other – painting, early writing skills, physical activities and **construction** can all be helpful.

---

### How we learn

To learn new concepts both children and adults move through three stages to transfer knowledge into long term memory:

1 The new **concept** is taught or explored.

2 It is practised with a teacher or alone.

3 The concept is used in play or work activities without further help.

# How you can help

**Parent tip**

"Talk about, practise and share activities with your child."

Activities and play at home can provide lots of **reinforcement** for new things learned at school. Everything you do with your child is part of the learning process.

✔ Give your time, especially to listen and talk.

✔ Take your child on visits to parks and other venues.

✔ Involve him or her in domestic tasks like cooking or cleaning.

Encourage early reading and maths skills at home. These areas have been targeted by the government as priorities. Children need help at home as well as good teaching at school to help them achieve targets appropriate for their age.

# Helping with reading

Reading is not about struggling through a reading scheme, being pushed on to ever harder texts because 'he can read this one too easily'.

It's very important that your child sees you reading for enjoyment as well as for a purpose, for example a magazine as well as the electricity bill. This teaches your child that books are fun as well as being learning tools. If you share books, read the stories many times before letting your child have a go by him or herself. Success is very important for children. They need to feel that they are progressing.

> ### Attitudes towards learning
>
> It is important that children come to school with the right attiude to reading.
>
> ✔ It should be fun.
>
> ✔ It should be interesting.
>
> ✔ It should be a normal part of their lives.

It's very good to talk about the pictures in the books – these are important clues to what is in the text. Give yourself enough time so that you can let your child retell the story in his or her own words. When reading together, point to the words as you read so that your child begins to understand the left to right pattern of reading. To give your child an overall interest in words, show him or her that books are only one sort of text. We can read signs, cereal packets, comics, words on TV and so much more – a visit to a supermarket or town centre can be just as stimulating as a library.

> ### Parent tip
>
> "Get a story book about going to the nursery or playgroup – make the situation sound familiar."

# Case study

## NIGHT TERRORS – AFRAID OF THE DARK

For several days Ricky's teacher had noticed he had been tired and bad tempered. He was also very reluctant to go to the toilet unless an adult went with him. Finally, at the end of the week, the teacher asked Ricky's mum to come in and have a chat. Ricky's mum had also been quite worried about him – for two weeks or more he had been waking up in the night screaming. When asked if he'd had a bad dream, he shook his head and cried. After this he refused to go back to sleep unless the light was left on. Ricky's teacher was aware that it is quite common for young children to wake up in the night, upset for no apparent reason. She arranged for Ricky and his mum to see the school nurse so that any problems could be talked over.

## ACTION

Ricky's mum was advised to keep calm when dealing with Ricky's 'night terrors'; to cuddle and reassure him and stay with him until he went back to sleep. Ricky was also given a night-light so that he was not afraid of the dark when he woke up.

> **Warning**
>
> There is some recent research evidence that permanent use of night-lights may be harmful to very young children's eyes, so their use should be phased out as the child returns to a more settled sleep pattern.

In class, the teacher read the children the story of 'The Train Who Was Afraid of the Dark'. She then encouraged all the children to talk about the things that scare them. Ricky told everyone that he didn't like the dark because 'there are monsters' in the darkness. Some of the children said there were monsters in the little corridor outside the toilets. In following story times the teacher read the children amusing stories about monsters and encouraged lots of talking about monsters being make-believe. She also arranged for the light outside the toilets to be left on. As the weeks went by, Ricky's bouts of 'night terrors' decreased.

# Books to read with your child

The range of books available for young children is extensive, and they are fun and exciting. Introduce your child to the library to explore what is available. The list given here has been chosen to introduce some favourite authors. The books have some particular talking points – colours, seasons, days of the week, rhymes, birthdays, behaviour and loss. These books will help your child to extend language and explore feelings.

## Books to read with your child

**Mick Inkpen**      **Kipper's Toybox**     **Hodder Children's Books**
**Kipper's Birthday**

The 'Kipper' series is a particular favourite with children. Illustrations are clear and text is short and easy to read together. These two books provide a starting point for talking about favourite things and celebrations.

**Michael Rosen & Arthur Robins**     **Little Rabbit Foo Foo**     **Walker Books**

An amusing book – for adults too – with wonderful illustrations. Little Rabbit Foo Foo provides a starting point for talking about good and bad behaviour or for just laughing together.

**Michael Rosen & Helen Oxenbury**     **We're Going on a Bear Hunt**     **Walker Books**

There is lots of repetition and plenty of action in this book and it is popular with children who love repeating rhymes. It is very good for talking about things that scare us and an excellent story for recalling and retelling.

**Eric Carle**     **The Very Hungry Caterpillar**     **Puffin Books**

A simple style is used to tell real facts through a story format. Growth and change are approached through a description of the butterfly's life cycle. Day and night, sequencing the days of the week and counting can all be taken from the story.

**John Prater**     **On Friday Something Funny Happened**     **Bodley Head**

Another amusing look at life from a child's eye view. Good for sequencing days and events and provides talking points about things we do, behaviour and being helpful.

**Pat Hutchins**  **You'll Soon Grow Into Them, Titch**  **Puffin Books**
A book about feelings and growing – how it feels to be the youngest and how a new baby changes things. The pictures cleverly reinforce the ideas about growing.

**Molly Bang**  **Ten Nine Eight**  **Puffin Books**
A straightforward book about ordering and recognising numbers and counting, which uses a different approach from just counting objects.

**John Burningham**  **Seasons**  **Red Fox**
This beautifully illustrated book is good for developing language related to colour, months and growth. Very helpful for explaining sequencing of the year, which children often find difficult.

**Mairi Hedderwick**  **Oh No, Peedie Peebles**  **Red Fox**
This book uses basic language and helps children to recognise colours in an interesting way.

**Jill Murphy**  **Peace At Last**  **Macmillan Children's Books**
Everyone who has to care for little children should read them this book – an amusing way of thinking about other people's need for their own time.

**Flora McDonell**  **I Love Animals**  **Walker Books**
Clear pictures and simple language help children to learn animal names and provide opportunities for talking about where they live, sounds they make and how to care for them.

**The Macmillan Treasury of Nursery Rhymes and Poems**  **Macmillan Children's Books**
A source of well-known nursery rhymes and children's poems for adults whose memories of these might have become a bit vague.

**Eileen Browne**  **Handa's Surprise**  **Walker Books**
Lovely pictures and simple text introduce children to a way of life outside Britain. Colour language can be reinforced and all sorts of differences can be talked about, including the weather.

**Sally Grindley &**  **Just Grandpa and Me**  **Dorling Kindersley**
**Jason Cockcroft**
A book that approaches the subjects of growing older and loss – issues that adults may find difficult to talk about when raised by young children.

**Lisa Stubbs**  **Sonny's Wonderful Wellingtons**  **Piccadilly**
A little story that explores the excitement of new and special things – and patience.

# Helping your child to write

Help your child to understand that there are lots of reasons for writing. Look at words on signs, lists, cards, invitations, letters, instructions on boxes – the examples are everywhere. Give your child lots of opportunities to develop his or her own play writing. This is an important stage before learning the correct letter formation.

## There are many different ways to encourage your child to write:

✔ Provide lots of paper in different sizes, colours and textures – wallpaper is good.

✔ Provide different sorts of crayons, pencils and safe (non-toxic) felt tips. At first children do best with 'chubby' crayons and pencils.

✔ Help your child to develop the correct, comfortable pencil grip by providing a triangular pencil or rubber pencil grip – these can be bought from toy shops or Early Learning Centres.

✔ Children need to explore mark making through scribbling, colouring in, drawing their own pictures and play writing to develop the controlled hand-eye co-ordination needed for proper writing.

*It's always helpful to talk to other parents and get their tips!*

When your child is beginning to write letters in his or her play writing you can start to teach the correct formation of each letter. Try these:

- ✔ tracing your child's fingers over textile letters or in sand

- ✔ tracing over your writing on paper

- ✔ handling plastic or wooden letters

- ✔ copying on the line below your own writing

- ✔ drawing or tracing patterns made up of the common strokes in writing – lines, circles, zig zags, loops and curves.

Always show your child the correct way to write from left to right and top to bottom.

Exercises such as these give your child practice in writing strokes.

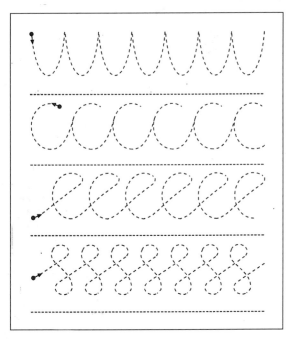

# Helping your child to count

Like words and letters, numbers are all around us and young children find them fascinating. Children should not just chant numbers in order without understanding that they mean 'how many of something'.

Make your child aware of numbers by finding them around the house or in the street:

- ✔ on clocks, timers, the TV control

- ✔ on car number plates

- ✔ on front doors

- ✔ on books and birthday cards

- ✔ on price tickets in shops

When teaching your child numbers, count things around you so that he or she begins to link the number words with objects.

# Helping with mathematics

Understanding that each number is 'one more than the one before' is quite hard for young children. They need lots of practice in counting and ordering numbers.

✔ Sing number rhymes together – Five Little Ducks, Ten Green Bottles.

✔ Play board games, such as snakes and ladders, that involve counting.

✔ When counting, adding on or taking away use visual cues – real objects or picture cards – to help your child's understanding.

✔ There are lots of opportunities during daily routines to introduce counting:
  • How many pieces of shredded wheat?
  • How many buttons do you have to do up?
  • How many stairs do you go up, can you count backwards coming down?
  • How many cars can we see?
  • How many people are waiting at the bus stop?

Early maths learning goes much further than counting skills.

## CHILDREN NEED TO UNDERSTAND:
  • shape and space – later they will learn geometry
  • patterns – later they will learn algebra
  • how to sort objects that have similarities into groups – later they will learn about data handling, graphs and diagrams

## Maths language

Children need to know maths language – how to express mathematical ideas in words and phrases such as:

• big and small, long and short

• heavy and light, full and empty

• add and subtract

• equals

• the names of shapes – square, rectangle, circle, triangle

ALL THESE THINGS CAN BE INTRODUCED INTO PLAY
AT HOME:

- ✔ building shapes and comparing big and small

- ✔ drawing round toys to look at their shape and putting them in order of size

- ✔ sorting clothes from the washing basket into colours or types, for example piles of socks or jumpers

- ✔ looking at strings of beads or patterns on curtains and clothing to see if they repeat or have special shapes

- ✔ sorting coins in your purse or wallet

- ✔ sorting a pack of playing cards into the suits or numbers

- ✔ putting two cards together and counting up the sum

*Don't put your children into playgroup too early. Give him or her a secure, loving background before rushing them out into the world.*

# Most importantly...

- ✔ be positive and keep learning experiences relaxed and happy
- ✔ praise all your child's efforts – even if he or she doesn't achieve at once – never criticise
- ✔ keep learning sessions short. Little children have short concentration spans. Ten minutes is often enough
- ✔ remember children are less responsive when they are tired – choose your time carefully

Education is a life-long process; it is about being able to enjoy learning new things. This enjoyment begins in the early years with parents, and with playgroups and nurseries.

*You are your child's best teacher*
*– you know him or her best.*

# Glossary

**Attainment Targets**   Targets for children's learning in each subject at different stages. Each attainment target is divided into eight levels, like steps up a ladder.

**Baseline Assessment**   Teacher observation of children within the first seven weeks of entering the Reception class, which is used to assess learning levels in maths, English and social skills.

**Concept**   A small piece of knowledge which helps us learn and understand new facts.

**Construction**   Activities involving putting things together, such as Lego, bricks or junk materials.

**Core subjects**   The main subjects in the National Curriculum: English, maths and science. R.E. (religious education) and I.C.T. (Information and Communications Technology) are also treated like core subjects. These are the only subjects where set Programmes of Study have to be taught in full.

**Early Years**   This refers to children's development from infancy (about 18 months) to six years when learning involves more reasoning and thinking skills.

**Early Years Outcomes**   The things children will have learned by the time they are five, published in Sir Ron Dearing's Report in 1996, 'Desirable Outcomes for Children's Learning on entering compulsory education'.

**Environment**   In this context it refers to pre-school surroundings, inside and outside, that promote learning and development.

**Foundation Subjects**   Subjects covered in schools as part of the National Curriculum which are not English, maths and science (the core subjects) or R.E. and I.C.T. These include history, geography, music, design technology, art and P.E.

**Information and Communications Technology (ICT)**   The term to replace I.T. (Information Technology) meaning the use of computers and other electronic means to enhance learning.

**Key Stages**   Stages at which a child's education can be assessed, after following a programme of work. There are four Key Stages, dividing ages 5-7, 7-11, 11-14 and 14-16.

**Key worker**   A staff member who has particular responsibility for befriending your child in the pre-school and for tracking his or her learning and needs.

**Literacy Hour**   The time each day which schools have to devote to teaching literacy skills.

**Local Education Authority (LEA)**   The county, borough or district education authority. LEAs have many specific roles especially in admissions, finance and special educational needs.

**National Curriculum**   The government's system of education broken down into four Key Stages, which applies to all pupils of compulsory school age in maintained schools. It contains core and foundation (non-core) subjects, and incorporates National Tests at the end of each Key Stage.

**National Tests**   Formerly known as SATS, these tests are taken in school at the end of each Key Stage – at ages 7, 11 and 14 – to determine what attainment targets pupils have reached. The scores are also used, especially at age 11, to compare the results of schools as a whole.

**PLA**   The Pre-School Learning Alliance.

**QCA**   The Qualifications and Curriculum Authority, who are responsible for all National Curriculum tests.

**Reinforcement**   Teaching children to repeat and practise tasks so that they can do them on their own.

**SEN**   Special educational needs.

**SENCO**   Special Needs Co-ordinator, a school's specialist.

**Spatial Awareness**   Being able to move the body efficiently; knowing about the size and area of physical space.

**Special needs**   This refers to the needs of any child who needs extra help or support to develop learning beyond that given to other mainstream children of the same age.

**Time out**   A method of discipline. The child is given five minutes or more away from the other children or given other activities to calm him or her down or prevent unwanted behaviour.

## USEFUL INFORMATION

**Action Aid**
CD-ROM 'Searching Stores'
A guide to multi-cultural stories from Africa, Asia and Latin America.
Web: www.actionaid.org/devedcat

**Advisory Centre for Education (ACE)**
Department A, Unit 1B Aberdeen Studios, 22 Highbury Grove, London N5 2DQ
Web: www.ace-ed.org.uk/
Phone: 020 7354 8321
Free advice, information and support for parents of children in state schools.

**Basic Skills Agency**
7th Floor, Commonwealth House
1-19 New Oxford Street, London
WC1A 1NU
Web: www.basic-skills.co.uk/
Phone: 020 7405 4017
National development agency for basic literacy and numeracy skills.

**British Association for Early Childhood Education (BAECE)**
136 Cavell Street,
London E1 2SA
Web: www.early-education.org.uk
Phone: 020 7539 5400

**DfEE (Department for Education and Employment)**
Sanctuary Buildings, Great Smith Street, London SW1P 3BT
Web: www.dfee.gov.uk
Phone: 0171 925 5000
Free publications on all aspects of education can be sent out, available by phoning
01787 880 946.

**Education Otherwise**
PO Box 7420
London N9 9SG
Web: www.e-o.users.netlink.co.uk/
Phone: 0891 518 303
For information about pre-school education at home, and general home education.

**National Association for Special Educational Needs**
NASEN House, 4/5 Amber Business Village, Amber Close, Amington, Tamworth B774RP
Web: www.nasen.org.uk
Phone: 01827 311 500

**National Confederation for Parent Teacher Associations (NCPTA)**
2 Ebbsfleet Estate, Stonebridge Road, Gravesend,
Kent DA11 9DZ
Web: www.rmplc.co.uk/orgs/ncpta
Phone: 01474 560 618
Promotes partnership between home and school, children, parents, teachers and education authorities.

**National Early Years Network**
77 Holloway Road,
London N7 8JZ
Phone: 020 7607 9573

**Pre-school Learning Alliance (PLA)**
69 King's Cross Road,
London WC1X 9LL
Web: www.childcare-now.co.uk/psla.html
Phone: 020 7833 0991

**TAMBA (Twins and Multiple Births Association)**
Harnett House, 309 Chester Road,
Little Sutton,
South Wirral L66 1QQ
Web: www.surreyweb.org.uk/tamba
Phone: 0870 121 4000

## WEBSITES

www.hometown.aol.com/wiseowlsw
A UK children's specialist in education software to play online or download.

www.bbc.co.uk/education/schools/primary.shtml
Home and school learning resources for children. The BBC education site as a whole has resources to cover a large range of educational issues.

## VIDEOS

**Getting Ready for School Video Guide**
Phone: 020 8444 9574

## OTHER PUBLICATIONS

Magazines such as Parent's magazine, Practical Parenting magazine and Nursery Nurse magazine have very useful and up-to-date information on pre-schools and pre-school children.